```
                              P
                              O
                              E
                              M
              ICONOGRAPHS
                              C
      I                       O
      C                       N
      O                       O
      N                       G
      O                       R
      G                       A
      R                       P
      A                       H
      POEMS
      H
      S
```

By May Swenson

ICONOGRAPHS

HALF SUN HALF SLEEP

POEMS TO SOLVE

TO MIX WITH TIME

A CAGE OF SPINES

ANOTHER ANIMAL

```
                M
                A
                Y

                S
                W
                E         ICONOGRAPHS            P
                N                 O              O              I
                S                 E              E              C
                O                 M              M              O
I  C  O  N  O  G  R  A  P  H  S                 SWENSON        N
                                                               O
                                                               G
                    POEMS                                      R
                    O     W                                    A
                    E     E                                    P
                    M     N                                    H
            ICONOGRAPHS   S                           POEMS
            C         O   O                           O
            O         E   N                           E
            N         M                               M
            O         S                        ICONOGRAPHS
            G                                  C
            R                                  O
            A     I                            N
            P     C                            O
            H     O                            G
            SWENSON                            R
                  O                            A
                  G                            P
                  R                            H
              CHARLES  SCRIBNER'S  SONS  .  NEW  YORK
                  P
                  H
                  S
```

A — 5.70 [MHO]

Printed in the United States of America
Library of Congress Catalog Card Number 70-85250

Acknowledgments

The following poems originally appeared in the magazines or
newspapers indicated below:

THE NEW YORKER
    Catbird in Redbud, Feel Me, Five Horses, The Lowering, The
    Power House, Seeing Jupiter, The Sunbird Settles To Its
    Nest, Unconscious Came a Beauty. Copyright © 1968, 1969
    May Swenson.

THE SOUTHERN REVIEW
    An Old Field Jacket, The Fingers, I Look At My Hand, How
    Everything Happens (Based on A Study Of The Wave), "Merry
    Christmas. You're On The Right," Notice, On Park Avenue At
    53rd Street, Orbiter 5 Shows How Earth Looks From The Moon,
    "Spring" by Robert Lowell (Photograph by Trudi Fuller), A
    Trellis for R. (under title, Blue).
    Copyright © 1969 May Swenson.

THE CARLETON MISCELLANY
    Over The Field, Wednesday At The Waldorf.
    Copyright © 1968 May Swenson.

CHICAGO TRIBUNE MAGAZINE
    Zero In The Cove.
    Copyright © 1970 May Swenson.

NEW AMERICAN REVIEW #3 (New American Library)
    Women.
    Copyright © 1968 May Swenson

THE NEW YORK TIMES
    Admire, Beginning To Squall.
    Copyright © 1968 May Swenson

4

Thanks is given by May Swenson to the Humanities and Social
Sciences Section of THE ROCKEFELLER FOUNDATION for a Fellowship
Grant which partly supported the work of this book.

```
I
C
C O N T E N T S
N
O
G
R
A
P
H
S
```

SECTION ONE

```
I
C
C O N T E N T S
N
O
G
R
A
P
H
S
```

SECTION TWO

SECTION ONE

ICONOGRAPHS

ONE

BLEEDING

Stop bleeding   said the knife.
I would if I   could said the cut.
Stop bleeding   you make me messy with this blood.
I'm sorry   said the cut.
Stop or   I will sink in farther said the knife.
Don't   said the cut.
The   knife did not say it couldn't help it but
it   sank in farther.
If   only you didn't bleed said the knife I wouldn't
have   to do this.
I know   said the cut I bleed too easily I hate
that I   can't help it I wish I were a knife like
you and   didn't have to bleed.
Well   meanwhile stop bleeding will you said the knife.
Yes you   are a mess and sinking in deeper said the cut I
will have   to stop.
Have you   stopped by now said the knife.
I've almost   stopped I think.
Why must you   bleed in the first place said the knife.
For the same   reason maybe that you must do what you
must do said   the cut.
I can't stand   bleeding said the knife and sank in farther.
I hate it too said   the cut I know it isn't you it's
me you're lucky to be   a knife you ought to be glad about that.
Too many cuts around   said the knife they're
messy I don't know how   they stand themselves.
They don't said the cut.
You're bleeding again.
No I've stopped said the cut   see you are coming out now the
blood is drying it will rub   off you'll be shiny again and clean.
If only cuts wouldn't bleed   so much said the knife coming
out a little.
But then knives might become   dull said the cut.
Aren't you still bleeding a   little said the knife.
I hope not said the cut.
I feel you are just a little.
Maybe just a little but I can   stop now.
I feel a little wetness still   said the knife sinking in a
little but then coming out a   little.
Just a little maybe just enough   said the cut.
That's enough now stop now do   you   feel better now said the knife.
I feel I have to bleed to   feel I   think said the cut.
I don't I don't have to   feel said   the knife drying now
becoming shiny.

WOMEN

```
Women                    Or they
    should be                should be
        pedestals                little horses
        moving                   those wooden
            pedestals            sweet
            moving                   oldfashioned
                to the               painted
                    motions          rocking
                    of men           horses
```

the gladdest things in the toyroom

```
            The                          feelingly
            pegs                         and then
            of their                     unfeelingly
            ears                     To be
            so familiar                  joyfully
            and dear                     ridden
        to the trusting              rockingly
        fists                        ridden until
    To be chafed                     the restored
```

egos dismount and the legs stride away

```
Immobile                 willing
    sweetlipped              to be set
        sturdy                  into motion
        and smiling          Women
            women                should be
                should always        pedestals
                be waiting               to men
```

THINGS I CAN DO IN MY SITUATION

1. I can shift my weight,
    eventually turn myself
        over.

            2. I can stretch
            my foot, touch
                the one
                    next to
                        me
                        (he
                        is
                        something
                    like a rock--)
                and attach myself
            to him.

            3. I can investigate the edges
        of my outer body, exude some moisture,
      and make the gesture of climbing out upon
    myself.

      4. Or, I can suck myself in tighter here, ignore
    the exposure to the light, relax in this position,
  uncomfortable as it is, and wait.

    The first is what I ought to do. That's why
        it occurred to me first. But this is the hardest. I have
            to thrust and turn, get my inner weight into motion,
                swivel around inside here, and reach outside-- although
                I'm attached to myself inside,
                at the deepest pinched point.
                I have literally to turn my inside out--
                    which is against my nature--
                        and then <u>heave</u> at the critical moment,
                            just before disequilibrium.
                                ...Risk of tumbling back and rolling...
                                downhill somewhere... of suffering
                                    trauma, and of getting lost...

                While I have been making these
                notes, the tide has been coming
              in, silently, reaching around
            and over the rocks.
              How could this
                happen so
                    quickly
                        and

secretly?
When I began
these notes-- it
seems only a moment ago--
lazy waves had barely begun
to touch the farthest rocks.
"Our rock"-- on which
we were born, I
suppose-- on
which we
have today
somehow been turned
upside down, our
tendernesses
exposed to
light--
is
already
being wetted
on all sides,
is shrinking in
top-room, and will
be entirely covered,
will vanish under water.

We are not prepared for this new
situation. I don't know about the
others, but I do not remember ever
being covered by the tide!
The little liquid I have in here of my
own-- can tide-water be anything like it?
In any case, it is all beyond my control.
What's worse, I am beyond my control. We
are stuck to this rock, which is stuck in
the sand, I suppose, and the swell of the
tide is going to obliterate it.

Now that it is too late, and there is nothing
I can do to restore my former situation, I am free
to withdraw my attention to myself
and to stop taking notice of what will happen.
Which has always been my natural state anyway...

As I again
take note, my
situation is much
as it used to be. The
rock is dry, is warm. I
am comfortable. Light strikes
the surface of the water far out.
I never used to notice that. I did
notice the warmth, against my foot--
supposed it came out of the rock. Light
comes from heat, which comes from above!
I have a good foothold. There is plenty
to eat. My lips have only to open
and something to eat squeezes its way
between them...

What happens happens again. And again.
   My companions are not the same ones.
     Maybe this rock is not the same one.
       But that is irrelevant...
         The tide comes in and goes out.
           Alternately wet and dry, wet and dry.
             A shock now and then. And afterward
               a trauma-nodule adds itself to the
                 others on my back.
                               I
                             have
                           not changed
                         in character,
                       only size, I think
                     with this accrual...

                     I seldom worry, or wish,
                       anymore. I no longer
                         even congratulate
                           myself on my
                             graduation
                               to near-
                                 perfect
                               sluggishness.
                     What continues to upheave
                   and recede cannot help itself
                 probably, anymore than I can.
               When it learns this, perhaps it will
             stop. When all expectation stops, perhaps
           then there will be a change. A real overturn!

I may be very large and heavy then, inside and outside. For instance,
   as large as this rock. Or larger. And it a nodule on my back?
     Suppose then I were to shift my weight?
       But I must forget that this occurred to me...
         I must stop these notes...
           It will be easy to shift, only if the memory of the
             possibility is dead...
               In order for it to happen, in fact, the
                 possibility must never have existed.

                 I will suck myself in,
                   forget that I am
                     growing...
                       the ludicrous
                         evidence
                               that...
                             ...that
                             space is
                           curved,
                         the universe a
                       snail.

OVER THE FIELD

          They have
          a certain
          beauty, those
          wheeled
fish, when over the field, steel fins stiff
          out from
          their sides,
          they grope,

          and then
          through cloud
          slice
          silver snouts,
          and climb,
trailing glamorous veils like slime.

Their long abdomens cannot curve, but
          arrogant cut
          blue, power
          enflaming

          their gills.
          They claim
that sea where no fish swam until they flew
          to minnow it
          with their
          metal.

The inflexible bellies carry, like roe,
          Jonahs
          sitting
          row on row.
          I sit by the
          fin, in

one of those whale-big, wheeled fish, while
          several silver
          minnows line
          up, rolling
          the runway way
          below.

EARTH WILL NOT LET GO

Earth will not let go our foot
except in her sea
cup she lets us float.

Thistle seed first parachute
and dragonfly the glider
use wind for skate.

So does flying squirrel
and helicopter humming
  bird and winged lizard. But wind

is earth's streamered wake
where she whirls and where
            in leather suit pterodactyl

and soaring albatross white yacht
proved not grace
 nor corpulance to extremes brought

breaks the sac earth wraps
her creatures in marsupial.
            "Only mammal capable of true

flight the bat"
equipped with sensory parts
            like modern instrument craft

swoops blind of blue
        unconscious a closet his orbit
or a cave construes

by echo which is radio.
For Icarus is not yet. The Wright
Aeroplane of 1903

was nothing but a big box kite
"in which the pilot lay prone
head forward his left hand

operating the lever his hips
in a saddle. Shifting
the hips sideways pulled

wires by which the wing tips
were warped and the rudder
 turned... a double action from one

movement controlling balance
     and direction." Blue pilot cap
cocked like kingfisher's beak

and heavy round-toed
            shoes how droll he wore.
Belly-down on the floor

of the long frail open
box he steered
 with his hips' wiggle. Not merely

the magic carpet
but the whole room
        he took with him trusting

   loops and fickle twists of air.
Lindbergh sat in a wicker chair
in The Cabin of the Spirit

and solo-crossed the Atlantic
in 1927. "...Impossible
to photograph the cabin in one view

  the actual distance from the back
of the seat to the face
of the instrument

board being only thirty-two
inches... His feet
        rested on the rudder control

pedals under the instrument
panel. To see ahead
        he either used the periscope

or steered to one side
while looking out the window."
        Enclosed in a sort of kayak

in wicker to save weight
the single wing his roof
              head bonneted and goggled

like a plucky scaup
            with swivelled neck he swam
on swells of ocean wind.

            Not unencumbered ever or by
muscle and buoyancy alone
may we climb loose

out of earth's rings
            her atmospheres ionospheres
the pastures to our lungs.

Rejecting wings
  props wheels for landing all bird
and insect things

John Glenn
      snug in the tip of a cartridge
was discharged in 1962

like a spore
            within its pod was launched
by blowgun of pure

energy. His lungfood
            he took with him. His suit
an embryonic sac

the capsule hugged him
uterus-tight. So tumbling
      backward by propulsion he tore

the planet's web to the edge.
But a last elastic caught him
 kept him to its circle. Implosion

    inbuilt homeward sucked him back
to splashdown in her sea cup
that salty womb

        that spewed the stillborn moon.
To that rock Apollo
astronauts would reach

they must take the earthpouch
  simulated. And it may not breach.
For earth will not let go

our foot though
                headfirst to be born
in angel space

we make wings
          jets rockets orbit tables
spider-landing legs.

THE DNA MOLECULE
THE DNA MOLECULE
THE DNA MOLECULE
is The Nude Descending a Staircase
a circular one.
See the undersurfaces
of the spiral
treads and
the spaces
in between.

She is descending and at the same time
ascending and she moves around herself. For
she is the staircase "a protoplasmic framework
an internal scaffolding
that twists and turns."

She is a double helix mounting and dismounting
around the swivel of her imaginary spine. The Nude
named DNA can be constructed as a model with matches and
a ribbon of tape. Be sure to use only 4 colors on 2 white
strands of twistable tape. "Only matches of complementary
colors may be placed opposite each other. The pairs
are to be red and green and yellow and blue."

Make your model as high as the Empire
State Building and you have an acceptable
replica of The Nude.
But and this is harder you must make her move
in a continuous coil
an alpha helix a double spiral
downward and upward at once
and you must make her increase while at the same
time occupying the same field.
She must be made "to maintain a basic topography"
changing yet remaining stable

if she is to perform her function which is to produce
and reproduce the microsphere.
Such a sphere is invisible to but ominpresent
in the naked eye of The Nude.
It contains "a central region and an outer membrane"
making it able to divide "to make exact copies of
itself without limit."

The Nude has "the capacity for
replication and transcription" of
all genesis. She ingests and
regurgitates the genetic material
it being the material of her own
cell-self. From single she becomes
double and from double single.

As a woman ingests the demon sperm and with the same membrane
regurgitates the mitotic double of herself upon the

slide of time so the DNA
pop at the waistline of its viscous drop
MOLECULE produces with a little
a new microsphere the same size
as herself which proceeds singly to grow
in order to divide and double itself.
So from single to double and double to single and
mounting while descending she proliferates while
expands while contracts she
disappearing at both of her ends.

Remember that red can only be opposite green
and blue opposite yellow. Remember that the
complementary pairs of matches must differ slightly in
length "for nature's pairs can be made only with units
whose structures permit an interplay of forces
between the partners."

I fixed a blue match opposite a red
match of the same length
in defiance of the rules pointed them
away from the center on the double-stranded
tape. I saw laid a number of eggs

on eggs on the sticky side of a twig.
I saw a worm with many feet grow out
of an egg.

The worm climbed the twig a single helix and gobbled
the magnified edge of a leaf
in quick enormous bites.

It then secreted out of itself a gray floss
with which it wrapped itself tail first and so on
until it had completely muffled
and encased itself head last as in a mummy pouch.

I saw plushy irridescent wings push
moistly out of the pouch. At first glued
together they began to part. On each wing

I saw a large blue eye
open forever in the expression of resurrection.
The new Nude released the flanges
of her wings
stretching herself to touch

at all points
the outermost rim
of the noösphere.

I saw that for her body from which the
wings expanded
she had retained
the worm.

I LOOK AT MY HAND

I look at my hand and see
      it is also his and hers;
   the pads of the fingers his,

                  the wrists and knuckles hers.
                  In the mirror my pugnacious eye
                     and ear of an elf, his;

                        my tamer mouth and slant
                              cheekbones hers.
                  His impulses my senses swarm,
               her hesitations they gather.
                  Father and Mother
                  who dropped me,

                  an acorn in the wood,
               repository of your shapes
         and inner streams and circles,

            you who lengthen toward heaven,
            forgive me
               that I do not throw

      the replacing green
      trunk when you are ash,
      When you are ash, no
   features shall there be,
tangled of you,
   interlacing hands and faces

         through me
      who hide, still hard,
         far down under your shades--

                  and break my root, and prune my buds,
                        that what can make no replica
               may spring from me.

I'LL BE

```
                                        Young,
                       I  was too   young
           to see and think and say: "I  am  young
                       I  am too   young."

                                        Old,
                       I  am too   young
           to see and think,  and say: "I  am  old,
                       I  was   young.
                       I  am too   old."

                                        Older,
                      I'll  be too   old
       to see,  and think,  and say: "I  was too   young,
                                too   old."

                                        Older,
                      I'll  be too   old
                     to...  I'll  be  dead,
                       too.  Be  dead
                          to...  Dead
                     I'll  be!  Dead,
                     I'll  be.
```

THE SHAPE OF DEATH

What does love look like? We know the shape of death.
Death is a cloud, immense and awesome. At first a
lid is lifted from the eye of light. There is a
clap of sound. A white blossom belches from the
jaw of fright. A pillared cloud churns from
white to gray, like a monstrous brain that bursts
and burns-- then turns sickly black, spilling
away, filling the whole sky with ashes of dread.
Thickly it wraps, between the clean seas and the
moon, the earth's green head. Trapped in its
cocoon, its choking breath, we know the shape
of death. Death is a cloud. What does love look

like? Is it a particle, a star, invisible entirely,
beyond the microscope and Palomar? A dimension past
the length of hope? Is it a climate far and fair,
that we shall never dare discover? What is its
color, and its alchemy? Is it a jewel in the earth,
can it be dug? Or dredged from the sea? Can
it be bought? Can it be sown and harvested? Is it
a shy beast to be caught? Death is a cloud-- immense,
a clap of sound. Love is little and not loud. It
nests within each cell, and it cannot be split. It
is a ray, a seed, a note, a word, a secret motion of
our air and blood. It is not alien-- it is near--
our very skin, a sheath to keep us pure of fear.

THE MOBILE
IN BACK OF THE SMITHSONIAN

glanced at is not realized
to be in motion.

Rotates so slowly silently twists
gradually mutates.

A steel ribbon an altering bow
on a pin on a tall triangle its black pediment.

Passing toward it around it antstreaming under it
on into the doorways or away they do

not notice
except as obstruction

perhaps decoration
what

is dismissed with
a shift to the

next objective
next object.

Or if they fasten
upon it their glances

take off.
their eyes inattentive

flick too quick to find it
moves.

Nor stop in the strolling cloud
of mind to claim how it

moves.
How slow how secret as time.

Never to follow its transforms to
count its changes

eyeflow with its outlines eyesit central
in its inspaces anticipate the uncurling

jointures of a figure forever unstable.
Never to know.

The bridge of Discover they do not lift an eye
to and climb

but crawl eyes across other eyes crawling where
others cross.

                    Automatic feet follow feet follow
                    groupmobile sightstoppered see-ers

              steered streaming to the Labels
              directed to collected at the Plaques the

          information Frames the strips of Print
          eyelevel.

        Not to the object but to the explanation of
        the object.

      Not to the mirror declaring the corridor of
      the pupil plunging straight horizontal a

    drawbridge into the palace of the mind
    where at the point of a triangle Universe

  unloops entwines unknots involutes
  coexistent beginsgrowsdiesendsbegins.

    But to the title on the bottom frame
    of the mirror the signature in the

        righthand corner to the type on the strip
        under glass beside the thing on the wall.

          To the bronze lettering on the base of the pediment.
          At which they have to stoop.

              A double deviational Mobius band of steel
              persuasively merges emerges expands in an

                  undefined sequence of changes.
                  An elegance unnoticed by no seam

                        deciding beginning
                        by no limit denoting end

                              or whether or if or where
                              is completion or source

                                  for its permutations.
                                  What without label

                                  rears invisible
                                  without sound below

                                  the speed of sight
                                  covertly turns.

                              Nor does the man at the
                              lobby desk know if you

                          ask him Who made it.
                          Too slowly for my eye

                              at first to see that it
                              moves

                         when I move
                         my pencil to diagram

                         its alterations it
                         moves

                         too fast to track
                         them all to trace

                         them a sidewinder
                         eluding all my

                         eye'shand's computations.
                    Now some of them notice

                    me motionless looking
               up at unnoticeable motion.

          They stop and look
     at me.

  And then at what I look
 at but then at me.

 And then at each other looking
 at me.

  And then at each other walking on walk on
          look back at me.

NOTE: The Mobile is by Jose de Rivera,
mounted outside the new wing of the
Smithsonian Institute in Washington, D.C.

Why do they say 31,000 feet? Why
not yards or miles? Why four
cigarettes and no match? Fly
Winston and see the world-- red, white,
filtered, slick in cellophane. We goose
our yellow corntips into the pink
leftover straw(sic)berry mousse
sequined with ash. Coffee comes
in a plasti-cup and sunlight
drills the rivets on the jet-
stream stack just inches beyond
the window and our nose, yet
the inner pane is cool, a breeze--
is it from outer space?--
pleasantly swizzles our face.

Is that St. Louis and the Gateway
to the West? Strident aluminum
hairpin the light tweaks down there.
No, no hairpins anymore. No
bobby pins. No
bobs. What do they call them, those
wire sausage things that build high hair?
Now sun is staining a cleft in cloud
like dogpiss on snow.

What do we do, our coffee's cold, it's
bumpy over Texas? Stewardess
wipes an old man's front, he spilled
his tray. We sneak to set
ours on the floor. The nose
lifts, bucks, beginning banking,
wing slips down. A shoe
ahead gets soaked under the seat,
the foot pretending sleep pretends
no notice. Maybe that's the U.
of Texas Tower, its stone prick due
visible in five minutes, which
would mean this mother'll be on time.
Around which how many people was it died?
Hope when the pilot circles
Austin we're on the right side.

The popcorn is greasy,
and I forgot to bring a
Kleenex. A pill that's a
bomb inside the stomach
of a man inside The
Embassy blows up. Eruc-
tations of flame, luxur-
ious cauliflowers, gigan-
ticize into motion. The
entire 29-ft. screen is
orange, is crackling
flesh and brick bursting,
blackening, smithereened.
I unwrap a Dentyne and,
while jouncing my teeth
in rubber-tongue-smart-
ing clove, try with the
2-inch-wide paper to
blot butter off my fingers. A bubble-
bath, room-sized,in which 14 girls,
delectable and sexless, are twist-
topped Creamy Freezes, (their
blond, red, brown, pinkish, lav-
endar or silver wiglets screw-
ed that high, and varnished)
scrub-tickle a lone male,
whose chest has just the
right amount and distri-
bution of not too curly
hair. He's nervously
pretending to defend
his modesty. His
crotch, below the
waterline, is
also below the
frame-- but unsubmerged
all 28 slick foamy boobs.
Their makeup fails to let
the girls look naked.
Caterpillar lashes, black
and thick, lush lips
glossed pink like the gum
I pop and chew, Contacts
on all the eyes that are
mostly blue, they're
nose-perfect replicas of
each other. I've got
most of the grease off and
on to this little square
of paper. I'm folding it
now, making creases with
my nails.

                              IT RAINS

          It rains
                    Write a rain   poem
          It stops
                    Write a stop   poem
              Shit
                    Write a shit   poem
      I love you
                    Write a love   poem
                Die
                    Write a dead   poem
          Fight
                    Write a fight poem
          Hate
                    Write a hate   poem
          Write
                    Write a write poem
            Wait
                    Make   a wait   poem
          Sleep
                    Sleep a   poem
              Wake   a   poem

                                                                    33

FEEL ME

"Feel me to do right," our father said
on his death bed. We did not quite
 know-- in fact, not at all-- what he meant.
His last whisper was spent as through a slot in a wall.
He left us a key, but how did it
fit? "Feel me
     to do right." Did it mean

that, though he died, he would be felt
    through some aperture, or by some unseen instrument
our dad just then had come
     to know? So, to do right always, we need but feel his
        spirit? Or was it merely
     his apology for dying? "Feel that I
     do right in not trying, as you insist, to stay

               on your side. There is the wide
          gateway and the splendid tower,
and you implore me to wait here, with the worms!"
          Had he defined his terms, and could we discriminate
          among his motives, we might
     have found out how to "do right" before we died-- supposing
          he felt he suddenly knew

               what dying was.
               "You do wrong because you do not feel
as I do now" was maybe the sense. "Feel me, and emulate
               my state, for I am becoming less dense--
          I am feeling right, for the first
time." And then the vessel burst, and we were kneeling
               around an emptiness.

          We cannot feel our
father now. His power courses through us, yes, but he--
     the chest and cheek, the foot and palm,
     the mouth of oracle-- is calm. And we still seek
          his meaning. "Feel me," he said,
     and emphasized that word.
     Should we have heard it as a plea

          for a caress-- A constant caress,
since flesh to flesh was all that we could do right
if we would bless him? The dying must feel
               the pressure of that
          question-- lying flat, turning cold
          from brow to heel-- the hot
          cowards there above

          protesting their love, and saying
               "What can we do? Are you all
                    right?" While the wall opens
          and the blue night pours through. "What
     can we do? We want to do what's right."
"Lie down with me, and hold me, tight. Touch me. Be
     with me. Feel with me. Feel me, to do right."

THE FINGERS

"If it moves you, move." The fingers
on the upturned bell-shaped glass, three strangers

to each other, waited. In an oval on the table
the alphabet, strung on squares from the Scrabble,

waited for the spirit to choose. Two signs,
like small grave-slabs, of paper with blue lines,

fixed YES and NO at the orbit's ends.
The fingers felt like fools together. The hands

separately trembled. Anticipation's cold
tickled the elbows. Willing to be fooled

wanting a happening, a three-part ghost
gathered itself under the glass from the moist

swirls of the fingertips. "Is anybody there?"
Alert for intentions, three pairs

of eyes, meeting above the lot
in the lamplight, declared no plot.

"Is anybody there? Let us know."
The giggling glass slid around to NO.

"Nobody there? But you're speaking.
Tell us if any of us here is faking.

"Spell out the name-- but first, answer if YES."
"G"-- the ghost walked out its word-- "U E S S."

Unlikely a king finger rode the joking throne.
Not acquainted till tonight, each felt pawn

to the others. But some compound sprite wanted
to rule, without detection from its "bodies," and hinted

at cheating as a distraction.
Would it produce some sort of resurrection?

"Let's ask it a personal question. What is a ghost
made of? What element is there most

like it? Tell us now, so we can understand."
The fingers throbbed as brothers on one hand,

that swept the glass out: It touched "B"
then stammered "L" and "O"-- "O" again, then "D."

Moved? We were so moved, we grew
hysterical. A poltergeist must have hopped aboard, too.

Jumping, the glass moved round to spell JUMPS, JUMPS-- until
it fell. BLOOD JUMPS is what the fingers had to tell.

ELECTRONIC SOUND

A pebble swells to a boulder at low speed
                    At 7½ ips a hiss is a hurricane.
                              The basin drain
is Charybdis sucking
                    a clipper down, the ship
                          a paperclip
whirling. Or gargle, brush your teeth, HEAR
                  a winded horse's esophagus lurch
                on playback at 15/16. Perch
a quarter on edge on a plate, spin:
            a locomotive's wheel is wrenched loose,
        wobbles down the line to slam the caboose,
keeps on snicking over the ties
                  till it teeters on the embankment,
                          bowls down a cement
ramp, meanders onto the turnpike
                        and into a junkhole
          of scrapped cars. Ceasing to roll,
it shimmies, falters...
                    sudden inertia causes
                          pause.
Then a round of echoes
                  descending, a minor yammer
as when a triangle's nicked by the slimmest hammer.

THE GRAIN OF OUR EYE (A Scientific Abstract)

Anti-matter it is called.
Awkwardness in naming the
   nonthing unnoticeably not
   occurring anywhere.
Mistaken to assume it (the
non-it) an unoccupant of
   nospace, a simple non-x-
   istent. No, it's (non-it's
not yes) the very grain
of our eye. As hair-crack
   in microscope adds x-tra
   leg to fly, proliferating
nonlegs in all inconsequent
offspring. Or subtracting
   an ex and so re-non-producing
   onspring. No is On by
mirror-proof, and Yes is
almost Eyes. A ton (or not
   notice) of anti-matter weighs
   (some ways, the sum's) the
same as empty sack of non-
feathers, and is the size
   of Between, which varies by
   a pivot (as on schoolboy's
compass) x-cept that this
tool's aim's to make ends
   meet meticulously in-x-act.
   What's its (non-its or nits)
anti-shape? Well, turn in
itside out and cross out
   out. Now print if you can't
   a non-positive pro-negative
of the after-image (or pre-
if-you-fer) of 0 in the
   word word, when warped by
   a million or so small but
unappreciable elisions,
collisions, incisions and
   noninverted visions between
   (between being the wee-in
intwixt the hole problem)
0 and the nonidentical
   rag content of unavoidably
   aging pages in that thick
folio entitled to no title
unless Void. We learn not
   how, but how Not, since

```
      one is almost own, knot
two.   (That's nearer out.)
To avoid a void, forget
    get, take care to be care-
    less.  Lesscare takes
development, requires a
dark room in the nonbrain
    that's tense, prehensile,
    unintentionally indented
with dense pre-eidetic non-
ideas.  Taodal blindness
    by its elf won't do.
```

SCIENCE AND RELIGION - A MERGER

When Galileo Galilei first turned a telescope on the heavens,
400 years ago, his revelations were astounding. Jupiter,
he found, has its own miniature system of planets,
or moons. He saw the mountains of the moon,
spots on the sun and the crescent shape of Venus.
He found that the Milky Way Galaxy
of which we are a part is actually formed from billions of
distant, dim stars. Since then, telescopes have gradually increased
in size and quality, culminating in 1948
in completion of the great reflector on Mount Palomar
in California. This instrument, with a parabolic mirror
200 inches in diameter, has been to modern astronomy what
Galileo's instrument was to science in the 17th Century.
It has carried man's ken toward the outer fringes
of the universe and it has enlarged his knowledge of the galaxies.
It first identified the strange quasars that seem to be the
most distant observable objects and the light-collecting power of

Was St. Peter buried on Vatican hill,
the site of the great Roman Catholic basilica
that bears his name? Last week Pope Paul....
gave his support to that theory, announcing that bones
discovered in 1953 under the basilica
had been identified to his satisfaction as those of
the saint. For Christians.... it is not an idle question...
The claims.... rest on two arguments
concerning Peter: First, that the statement
of Jesus quoted by Matthew: "Thou art Peter, and
upon this rock I shall build my church"
is literally true... and second, that the apostle
Peter was bishop of Rome, and thus the first
in an unending series of Roman bishops--or--popes,
who embody the full authority to guide
the Christian Church. In 1939, the
Vatican excavations beneath the main altar of St. Peter's

its huge mirror has brought into view peculiar stars,

    began to uncover a series of tombs, which

that, while not very distant, are too dim to be observed with

    was held to include the tomb of Peter. But

other instruments.... While others are being built, none comes close to

        the first announcement

the 200-inch Hale Telescope-- with one exception. That is

    came only in 1949, when Pope Pius XII stated that

the 236-inch reflector being built by the Soviet Union near Zelenchuk

    an urn containing the remains of the apostle

in the Caucasus.... Apparently the Russians hope to dazzle the world

    had been uncovered.... Later, however, the bones

as they did with their Sputnik in 1957, by a surprise announcement after

    in the urn were shown to be those of a woman.

their first look into realms previously beyond reach....

    During the 1950's, Professor Margherita Guarducci,

While the Russians, with their new instrument, will be able to see things

    a Vatican expert on inscriptions, argued that

no one else can, their field of view will be limited by

    writings on walls beneath the altar pointed to

their geography.... Because almost all of the world's great observatories

    a particular niche as the resting place

are north of the Equator, the southern part of the sky

    of Peter's remains. Earlier a team of Vatican archeologists

is by far the least explored. The center

    had reported secretly to the Pope that the niche,

of the Milky Way Galaxy lies there

    and a box in it, were empty. But Professor Guarducci--

plus the two nearest baby-galaxies (the Clouds

    persisted, reporting that Monsignor Kaas, then secretary

of Magellan).... One of the dreams of American astronomers

    and administrator for the Fabric of St. Peter's, told her

is the placing of a large telescope

        that he and two workmen had removed some bones

into orbit above the earth's atmosphere.

        from the niche without the knowledge of Vatican

This has become possible with the giant Saturn rockets designed to send men to the moon. Our present view of the heavens can be likened to that of a lobster beneath the murky waters of Long Island Sound. A telescope above the ocean of air would open new realms of knowledge concerning our nearest neighbors in space, as well as the nature of the universe as a whole. However, as with other grandiose science projects, the problem is cost.... American action may be delayed until the Russians have done it first.

European archeologists familiar with the Vatican diggings remain privately skeptical but publicly silent.... Further investigations will likely be colored by the Pope's decision to commit some of his prestige to a circumstantial argument the bones in question are indeed Peter's. The Vatican has got itself into a position where its case can't be proved scientifically,' an American archeologist.. said last week. Ile said, "We'll probably never know whose bones they are."

It was these bones that Pope Paul archeologists. last week identified as those of St. Peter.

Note: The text is taken verbatim (except for deletions where indicated) and inter-woven from two columns by Walter Sullivan and John Leo, respectively, in the New York Times of Sunday, June 30, 1968, p. 10-E.

                The
                POWER
                HOUSE

                Close to my
                place is the
                power house.
                I knew there
                wouldn't be
                anybody in it.
                It's beauti-
                ful. Like a
                church. It
                works all by
                itself. And
    .   with almost no
                sound. All glass.
                And a tall square
                tower on it.
                Colored lights
                shine from within.
                They color the
                glass. Pink. Pale
                green. Not stained.
                Not that kind. And
                not fragile. Just
                light. Light weight.
                   A red rod erect
                   from the tower
blinking on top red. Behind it gray wings of motion. A fan
of light opening and folding somewhere in the west of town.
Periodic as a metronome.
The crickets were talking electricity. A white Spitz barked
at me though my sneakers made no noise. I walked up the
slight slope-- it's wide-- to the power house. Went past
the doorway. Big as a barn door squared. Big horse I thought.
I saw through the doorway gray metal coils. All the clean
machinery and engines. I don't know what to call it all. I
don't know the names.
   Painted pretty colors slick and clean. I knew there
wouldn't be anybody there. Nobody needs to work there
I thought. And walked past that door farther on.
   White lights icy and clean. Not blazing. Cool.
Gossamer. The pink and green like-sherbet-colors bathing the gray machines.
Came to a place where vapor cooled my skin. A breeze made by waterspray
up high. And there was white steam unfurling
   evaporating against the dark.
Down lower a red transparent ball on a pedestal. Incandescent. Big. A
balloon mystery. Inside through another doorway I saw a hook painted
yellow. Huge and high enough to lift a freight car.
   I stood looking in-- my shadow so long and black
from the streaming lights.
                And I was wrong. Somebody moved in the powerhouse.
                Came from between the coils and giant tubes.
                Down off the balcony on the steel stairway smooth
                and slow. Like floating. Like not having to
                look or think. I thought he'd be a Negro but he
                wasn't. He didn't see me. Didn't need to see
                anything. He had a red face and a blue uniform.

ORBITER 5 SHOWS
HOW EARTH LOOKS FROM THE MOON

There's a woman in the earth, sitting on
her heels. You see her from the back, in three-
quarter profile. She has a flowing pigtail. She's
holding something -- some holy jug. Her left arm is thinner,
in her right hand.

light swirling up out of her vessel. She's the Indian Ocean. Asia is
and her dancer's arm is the Suez Canal. Her pigtail points to Europe
in a square kimono, beneath the tip of Africa. She is a woman
bare feet tucked the Arabian Peninsula.

in a gesture like a dancer.

Her tail of long hair is

A woman in the earth.

A man in the moon.

Note: A telephoto of the earth, taken from above the moon by Lunar Orbiter 5 (printed
in The New York Times August 14, 1967) appeared to show the shadow-image of "a woman
in a square kimono" between the shapes of the continents. The title is the headline
over the photo.

BLACKTUESDAYBLACKTUESDAYBLACKTUESDAYBLACKTUESDAYBLACKTUESDAYBLACKTUESDAYBLACKTUESDAY

Blessèd is the man of color
for his blood is rich with
the nuclear sap of the sun.
Blessèd is his spirit which
a savage history has
refined to intercept
whitest lightnings of
vision. Blessèd the neck
of the black man made
muscular by the weight of
the yoke made proud
bursting the lynch rope.
Blessèd his body meek on
the slave block thunderous
on the porch of revolt.
Blessèd his head hewn with
animal beauty for he has
grappled as the lion bled
as the lamb and extracted
the excellence of each for
his character. Blessèd the
black and the white of his
eye.

For Martin Luther King
April 4, 1968

THE LOWERING*

The
flag
is folded
lengthwise,
and lengthwise
again,

folding toward the
open edge,
so that the union of stars
on the blue
field remains outward in full view;

a triangular folding is then begun
at the striped end,
by bringing the corner of the folded edge
to the open edge;
the outer point, turned inward

along the open edge,
forms the next triangular fold;
the folding continued so, until the end is reached,
the final corner tucked between
the folds of the blue union,
the form of the folded flag

          is found to resemble that
          of a 3-cornered pouch, or thick cocked hat.
          Take this flag, John Glenn, instead of a friend;

instead of a brother, Edward
Kennedy, take this flag;

instead of a father, Joe
Kennedy, take this flag;
this flag instead of a husband, Ethel
Kennedy, take this flag;

this 9-times-folded
red-white-striped, star-spotted-blue flag,
tucked and pocketed neatly, Nation,
instead of a leader, take

this folded flag. Robert
Kennedy, coffin without coverlet,

beside this hole in the grass,
beside your brother, John
Kennedy, in the grass,
take, instead of a country,
this folded flag;
Robert

Kennedy, take
this hole
in the
grass.

*Arlington
Cemetery
June 8,1968

45

AN OLD FIELD JACKET

At the Army Surplus Store I bought an old field jacket,
   because of the snapdown pockets and the attached hood
   rolled up and zippered inside the collar. Good
      for fishing, camping, wet days on the beach.
      Wrinkled, buckled, faded to swamp-mud-green,
         the harsh cloth's wonderfully softened, sateened
         by wear and machine cleaning.

         Sticky resinous marks still on it, above the breast
         pockets and on the arms, are where ID patches, chevrons,
      and whatnot, were ripped off. A blue-white phosphorescent strip
   sewn down the back, when it walks in the dark, still glows.

   Has it single-filed on sinister muck and brush patrols,
      hunched in hot foxholes? Has the hood
      under a hard hat heard mortar rain?
         For all I know, it used to smell of cold
            gun grease, cartridge powder, maybe blood. Smears of paint,
               or something, are on it, and other not quite washed out stains.

         It's loose on me, practical, a good
            wind-breaker, and not too long.
         Came cheap, and will last forever, the cloth's that strong.
         But the best is those four big pockets
      to keep cigarettes and matches dry
   in, carry car keys, flashlight, a fishknife, sinkers and bait--
a bird book, even-- anything I want.

Don't know why it fits my shoulders. Must have shrunk
   getting processed, disinfected, drycleaned for
      the Army Surplus Store. Wonder who wore
         it, and what for? A label by the hang-up loop in the lining says:
         <u>Cotton OG 107 Mil-J-4883C US Army</u>-- and then <u>September 1962</u>.

         Don't know how near it came to a shooting war--
            and wearing it, I hope, is the closest I'll ever get--
         women not being drafted yet.
(But if we start using their garb, is that what we're asking for?)

Standing up out of a tent into the rain
   this summer, Montauk or Maine--
      taking a lungful of dark before light,
         tying the drawstring on the hood,
            out in the open, feeling equipped, protected good,
               I might say:
                  Let's start the dirty day
                     early. Let's imagine military dawn.

SPRING BY ROBERT LOWELL (PHOTOGRAPH BY TRUDI FULLER)

...only an ear is in the spring.

                    Sunlight in Central Park it could
                  be:yond his shoulders the bench back
                a field for play: that's over
              exposed as video: fuzzy. Or is it Boston
          Common: maybe May be:hind him?
          Well: well light's be:hind him. Gray
        shades his face: is it a tree
      trunk's toppled roots' dark riot he sees
    casts shadow on him: be:fore him? Only

                    an ear and flesh of part
                  of a neck in sunlight: some
                of the right side of his shirt. A wish
              bone drawing pinches brows:
            parenthe-seizes lips: the eyes
          dim be:cause of shadow: not him:
        fright light white tight
      pellets in pupils: absent in photo

      flash his gaze that must be:spectacled.
        Be:fore head shows a setting
      sun reflected: light's spot on wavelet
    thought not sinking yet. A warm
  ear's drinking infant
light. Be:side him's morning in the spring
  Park: a hot beam rubbing the right
side of his dark coat: baring
as if a gray breast there.

NOTICE

(On reading Paul Goodman's poem in The New York Review, 9/14/67)

Now we are talking
straight out to each other,
and for all to hear.
The common stream of our heads (our heart)
till now compartmented
perhaps begins to combine. Maybe to flow
unsurreptitiously together,
unembarassed to know
we are one body (human)
helplessness and potency
the same circulation systeming
our veins. Paul Goodman
(well known, whom I don't know, and know
so well) breathing and thinking with you
in the same current (electric placenta
we all feed into, drink out of,
charger of every brain,
all blood) just now right here, I read
(with all the others who read)
your poem-prayer
on the death of your son,
so soon on reading
of his death, in the news. Then falling
(with him, with you, with all
the others who fall) a constant
mystery, the mountain down,
again I notice: Since mind first noticed
death, we fall. And how all
feel it (and conceal it)
the same tick-away, our massive
common heart in labor day after day.
Daring from now, perhaps,
to let go,
(the pretence of separate cells,
privacies, prides, singularities) let flow
away, like you, Goodman, we
(who are you, as you are us) may
(in the crack of recognition hurtling) publish
a piece of that heart.

MAsterMANANiMAl

ANiMAte MANANiMAl MAttress of Nerves

MANipulAtor Motor ANd Motive MAker

MAMMAliAN MAtrix MAt of rivers red

MortAl MANic Morsel Mover shAker

MAteriAl-MAster MAsticAtor oxygeN-eAter

MouNtAiN-MouNter MApper peNetrAtor

iN MoNster MetAl MANtle of the Air

MAssive wAter-surgeoN prestidigitAtor

MAchiNist MAsoN MesoN-Mixer MArble-heAver

coiNer cArver cities-idols-AtoMs-sMAsher

electric lever Metric AlcheMist

MeNtAl AMAzer igNorANt iNcubAtor

cANNibAl AutoMANANiMAl cAllous cAlculAtor

Milky MAgNetic MAN iNNoceNt iNNovAtor

MAlleAble MAMMAl MercuriAl ANd MAteriAl

MAsterANiMAl ANd ANiMA etheriAl

M = 52
A = 73
N = 40

                    t h e   B E A M

How things really are we would like to know.
Does
          T i m e
                    flow, is it elastic, or is it
atomized in instants hammered around the
     clock's face? And
                              S p a c e ,
                                        is it
     what we find around us in our place, or
     "a symbol, suitably haunted, of the

     M i n d?"
                    The
                         Mind?
                                   A beam
       fitfully focused, then dragged on. So
     all material in its ken is lit,
               consistent, tranquil as far as
     that visitation lasts. When it is
          withdrawn, when all we think and
       know "goes out" where does it go? Into
     a blind sink? No. It must find and drag
       into its circle new material for its
          being. Moving by
                         M i n d ' s
                                   light,
       which is slow,
                    M i n d
                              must move and warm
     the groove, spot particles for another
          seeing.

I'll rest here in the bend of my tail
said the python having traveled
his own length
beginning with his squared snout
laid beside his neck
O where does the neck

end and the chest begin
O where does the stomach
end and the loins begin
O where are the arms and legs
Now I'll travel between myself
said the python lifting his snout

and his blue eyes saw lead-gray
frames like windows on his hide
the glisten of himself the chill
pattern on each side
of himself and as his head slept
between the middles of himself

the end of his outer self still crept
The python reared his neck and yawned
his tongue was twins his mucous membrane
purple pink hibiscus sticky
He came to a cul de sac in the lane
of the center of his length

his low snout
trapped between twin windowed
creeping hills of himself
and no way out
I'll travel upon myself said the python
lifting his chin to a hill

of his inner length and while
his neck crossed one half of his
stomach his chest crossed his
loins while his tail lay still
But then he thought
I feel uncomfortable in

this upright knot
and he lowered his chin
from the shelf of himself
and tucked his snout in
How get away from myself said
the python beside himself

traveling his own side
How recognize myself as just myself
instead of a labyrinth I must travel
over and over stupified
His snout came to the end
of himself again to the final leaden bend

of himself
Said the python to his tail
Let's both rest till all
the double windowed middle maze
of ourself
gets through crawling

SECTION TWO

ICONOGRAPHS

          Unconscious
        came a beauty to my
      wrist
    and stopped my pencil,
   merged its shadow profile with
  my hand's ghost
 on the page:
 Red Spotted Purple or else Mourning
Cloak,
paired thin as paper wings, near black,
were edged on the seam side poppy orange,
 as were its spots.

UNCONSCIOUS

CAME A BEAUTY

I sat arrested, for its soot haired
body's worm
shone in the sun.
It bent its tongue long as
 a leg
  black on my skin
   and clung without my
   feeling,
     while its tomb stained
       duplicate parts of
         a window opened.
           And then I
             moved.

55

   !   !   ! !
CATBIRD IN REDBUD

  !   !   ! !
Catbird in the redbud this morning.
   ! ! !
No cat could
   !   !   ! !   !
mimic that rackety cadenza he's making.
  !   !
And it's not red,

the trapeze he's swaying on.

After last night's freeze,
  ! !   !   !
redbud's violet-pink, twinkled on
              !
by the sun. That bird's
  !   !
red, though, under the tail
              !
he wags, up sharply, like a wren.
     !   !
The uncut lawn hides blue
            !
violets with stargold eyes on the longest

stems I've ever seen. Going to

empty the garbage, I simply have
    !
to pick some,

reaching to the root of green,
           !
getting my fist dewy, happening
          ! !
to tear up a dandelion, too.
  !
Lilac, hazy blue-
         !   !
violet, nods buds over the alley
     ! !
fence, and (like a horse with a yen
               !
for something fresh for breakfast)

I put my nose into a fragrant

pompom, bite off some, and chew.

GEOMETRID

                    Writhes, rides down
                    on his own spit,
                    lets breeze twist

                    him so he chins,
                    humps, reels up it,
                    munching back

                    the vomit string.
                    Some drools
                    round his neck.

                    Arched into a staple
                    now, high on green
                    oak leaf he punctures

                    for food, what
                    was the point
                    of his act? Not

                    to spangle the air,
                    or show me his trick.
                    Breeze broke

                    his suck,
                    so he spit
                    a fraction of self's

                    length forth, bled
                    colorless from within,
                    to catch a balance,

                    glide to a knot
                    made with his own mouth.
                    Ruminant

                    while climbing, got
                    back better than bitten
                    leaf. Breeze

        that threw
    him snagged him
to a new.

57

ROUGH TRIPLETS

MY FACE THE NIGHT

My eyes seeing nothing
but night in my head
sent two tears south

toward inlets of my mouth.
                North in the height
there swam forth two stars

        as if from far pupils,
My tongue licked up two
salt drops of light.

ADMIRE

Amphibian bird and mammal cannot shine
            by own light as can some uglies
            of the undersoil and brine: Chill

        toadstool clam and worm. But one bug
            of fire's wink and sprinkle's printed
            higher on the chart of night. Why?

Mammals think that cannot shine. Admire
            the airy faery firefly. Know
one grub aglow a blink above the mire.

WHAT'S SECRET

Always the belly lighter than the back.
What grows in the shade pales,
what's secret keeps tender.

Inversion saves the silk of innocence.
Fierce melanosis of the adult coat
from whips of sun. The overt coarsens,

stripes and grins with color.
Exposure, experience thicken half the beast
who, shy as snow, stays naked underneath.

ROSIGNOLE TO THE CRITIC

Cats have only
their lives to save, while we
our souls (this means our

egos) must keep unslain. Power,
soul's blood, let from some slit
(a stab unnoticed until infected, it

made by the claw of Sneak,
the Cat) may leak
long poison, become a pustulate of self-hate,

paralyze the wings
and lock the little jaw
of Rosingnole that sings.

WINDOW IN THE TAIL

```
Nap of cloud                ion not
as thick                 of feather
as stuff-                       but
ing tight                     slat-
pack-                    ted alum-
ed for                         in-
a mat-                          um
tress tick-               or other
ing pick-
anin-                         met-
ny kin-                   al man-
ked and puff-            euverable
ed and white               by am-
as kid-                   ple ram-
shear-                    ps that
ed bel-                       bevel
ly ruff              up or slide
                          out wide
is the floor             and glide
and is the ceil-         our car-
ing o'er                  riage level
which we're
keel-                         Over
ed and sail-                   fur
ing on flat               of cloud
pin-                     we travel
```


Nap of cloud, as thick as stuffing
tight packed for a matress ticking,

     pickaninny kinked and puffed
and white as kid-sheared belly ruff,

     is the floor and is the ceiling
over which we're keeled and sailing,

     on flat pinion-- not of feather--
     but slatted aluminum or other

          metal maneuverable
     by ample ramps that bevel

     up, or slide out wide
          and glide

     our carriage level.
Over fur of cloud we travel.

ON PARK AVENUE AT 52nd STREET

```
    Spirits            Each              They
      are            strains            lurch
    dancing            to              laughter
      here--           be               and
      are            whitest,           hiss
    forced            most             wind
      to             festive,            white
      dance.       effervescent,         as
    They             tossing             the
      are            sparks             north.
      forced         and                Their
      up               gouts,           force
    out             white              is
    of                "works         perpetual
    brass             of                mirth,
rectums.            fire."               pressed

      Pressed        Throwing           out
    from              up                of
      rigid          their             brass
    slits,            heads,          rectums.
      they            they             They
    shoot            catch          juggle
      tall,           their             the
    out             heads            globulous
    of                on               white
    the             shoulders     expectorations,
      floor          they             the
    of                form             flakes
    their            over            of
      dark            and              their
      basin.          over.            heads.
```

61

"MERRY CHRISTMAS. YOU'RE ON THE RIGHT."

I'm looking at those two raffish child-angels
by Raphael, a section of his sky this corner
transaction cropped for close-up on a picture card.
Sunwarmed, well-fleshed, naked except for wings,
(the plum-red bows unpleating from their shoulder-blades,
so short they couldn't hold a robin up, are pure

convention), they rest their elbows on a beam
that looks like wood, not light-- some plank in middle
heaven they've seized for perch, or, breaking surface,
        reached arms up over, like a raft or rafter. There
        they dawdle, hips immersed, unseen from behind,
        kissed, blown on, spanked by waves that could be either

        wind or water. The object they contemplate in the high
        foreground they're free to imagine, since it's out
        of view: a new assumption, ritualistic but not serene,
that will not set, nor need it tarnish noticeably.
(I'll paint it so, as were those two angels in impudent
postures long ago.) Beatitudinally turned aloft,

the eyes, of the one with ruffed hair, chin in hand,
look devil-wise. Innocence on the round brow
and quirky mouth of the other's a mask, no doubt,
        for cupid acts practiced toward the dart board's center,
        simultaneous with the stare of adoration. The canvas
        being infinite, how relatively small or large is this

        detail? Dimensions are, in fact, neglected on the card,
        the frame that snares and magnifies encounter into
        permanence. From in front, two plump, spunky angels
seem intent (while carefully not looking at each other)
on adoring whatever I choose to place up there,
their propinquity accidental. Well, angels need no

conscience. The mysterious rail (the color of altar cloth
I suddenly realize) is charged. Between elbow and naked
elbow's a light-gap, electric white. And, in the gray-blue
        robelike flowing of cloud inflations far out, a green
        brush-streak seems to brighten-- a freezing omen. Have
        the angels just heard thunder? Or are they about to hear?

A TRELLIS FOR R.

```
B
L
U
E but you are R
             o
             s
               e too
and buttermilk but with blood
dots showing through.
A little salty your white

nape boy-wide.  Glinting hairs shoot
back of your ears' R
                   o
                   s
                     e that
tongue likes to feel
the maze of slip into
the funnel tell a thunder whisper to.
When I kiss

your eyes' straight lashes
down crisp go like doll's
blond straws.  Glazed
iris R
     o
     s
     e
     s your lids unclose
to B
   l
   u
   e ringed targets their dark
sheen spokes almost green.  I sink in
B
l
u
e black R
         o
         s
           e heart holes until
you blink.
```

```
Pink lips the serrate
folds taste smooth
and R
    o
    s
    e
    h
    i
    p round the center
bud I suck.  I milknip

your two B
         l
         u
            e skeined blown R
                            o
                            s
                            e
beauties too to sniff their
berries' blood up stiff pink tips.
You're white

in patches only mostly R
                        o
                        s
                        e
buck skin and salty
speckled like a sky.  I
love your spots your white neck R
                                o
                                s
                                e
your hair's wild straw splash
silk spools for your ears.
But where white spouts out spills

on your brow to clear
eyepools wheel shafts of light
R
o
s
e you are B
           l
           u
           e.
```

WEDNESDAY AT THE WALDORF

```
   ɪ         +              :
```
Two white whales have been installed at

```
      :
```
The Waldorf. They are tumbling slowly

```
           +
```
above the tables, butting the chandeleirs,

```
              +      :
```
submerging, and taking soft bites

```
            =    =      +
```
out of the red-vested waiters in the

```
      :     ɪ
```
Peacock Room. They are poking <u>fleur de lis</u>

```
   +              :    :
```
tails into the long pockets on the

```
   +
```
waiters' thighs. They are stealing

```
    =          :                ɪ =   =
```
breakfast strawberries from two eccentric

```
       =                              :
```
guests-- one, skunk-cabbage-green with dark

peepers-- the other, wild rose and

```
                =           : + =
```
milkweed, barelegged, in Lafayette loafers.

```
          ɪ    =    =        = = +
```
When the two guests enter the elevator,

```
       +        =              ɪ    :
```
the whales ascend, bouncing, through all

the ceilings, to the sixth floor. They

```
    =
```
get between the sheets. There they turn

candy-pink, with sky-colored eyes, and

                    :   =   =
silver bubbles start to rise from velvet

    +   :   =
navels on the tops of their heads.

    +   +   Ι   Ι   =
Later, a pale blue VW, running on poetry,

              :   =
weaves down Park Avenue, past yellow

                              Ι   Ι   Ι
sprouts of forsythia, which, due to dog-do

        Ι   Ι   Ι
and dew, are doing nicely. The two

            +   Ι   :
white whales have the blue car in tow

          +   +
on a swaying chain of bubbles. They are

                      =
rising toward the heliport on the Pan Am

    Ι
roof. There they go, dirigible and slow,

                              +
hide-swiping each other, lily tails flipping,

            =   =
their square velvet snouts stitched with

                  +
snug smiles. It is April. "There's

              :
a kind of hush all over the world."

IN THE YARD

Dogwood's s n o w. Its ground's air.
R e d h e a d e d's riddling the phone pole.

Fat-tailed she-dog grinning's
t h r a s h e r - r e d.

It's the oriole there by the feeder
c h e d d a r under b l a c k bold head.

Neighbor doing yardwork's getting r e d.
Lifts tiles to a barrow.

L.I.R.R.'s four cars rollskate by
w h i t e potato blooms farside the field.

That square's our bedroom window.
You're not there. You're away

looking for nails or such
to put up a mirror frame the Adam

and Eve bright hair held back by a
r o b i n's - e g g - b l u e band.

Or you're at the body shop about
the broken bumper.

C a b b a g e b u t t e r f l y's found
h o n e y he thinks on r i n g

g l i n t s on my hand. I wait
for the r i n g n e c k who

noseblows twice parades his mate. She's g r a y.
Until comes the B l u e Bug crunching driveway.

You're back barefoot brought some fruit.
Split me a n a p p l e. We'll get r e d

w h i t e halves each our
juice on the Indian spread.

                    THE YEAR OF THE DOUBLE SPRING

        Passing a lank boy, bangs to the eyebrows, licking a Snow Flake cone,
cones on the tulip tree up stiff, honeysuckle tubelets weighting a vine,
and passing Irene Gay - Realtor, The Black Whale, Rexall, and others-- (Irene,

                    don't sue me, it's just your sign I need in the scene)--
      remembering lilac a month back, a different faded shade, buying a paper
with the tide table instead of the twister forecast on page three,

then walking home from the village, beneath the viaduct I find
                    Midwest echoes answering echoes that another, yet the same
   train wakes here out East. I'm thinking of how I leaned on you, you leaning

in the stone underpass striped with shadows of tracks and ties,
and I said, "Give me a kiss, A.D., even if you are tranquilized," and I'm
            thinking of the Day of Shooting, the Day of the Kingfisher, the Indigo

      Day of the Bunting-- of the Catfish Night I locked the keys in the car
                and you tried to jimmy in, but couldn't with a clothes hanger.
The night of the Juke at Al's-- When Something's Wrong With My Baby--

you pretended to flake out on the bench, and I poured icy Scotch into
the thimble of your belly, lifting the T-shirt. Another night you threw up
                in a Negro's shoe. It's Accabonac now, instead of Tippecanoe.

      I'm remembering how we used to drive to The Custard "to check out the
                teenage boxes." I liked the ones around the Hondas, who
from a surly distance, from under the hair in their eyes, cruised the girls

in flowered shorts. One day back there, licking cones, we looked in
on a lioness lying with her turd behind the gritty window of a little zoo.
                              I liked it there. I'd like it anywhere with you.

    Here there are gorgeous pheasants, no hogs, blond horses, and Alec Guiness
              seen at The Maidstone Memorial Eve-- and also better dumps. You
scavenged my plywood desk top, a narrow paint-flecked old door

the broad white wicker I'm sitting in now. While you're at the dump
hunting for more-- maybe a double spring good as that single you climbed to
          last night (and last year)-- I sit in front of a house, remembering

          a house back there, thinking of a house-- where? when?-- by spring
        next year? I notice the immature oak leaves, vivid as redbud almost,
and shaped like the spore of the weasel I saw once by the Wabash.

Instead of "to the Readmore" riffling Playboy, I found you yesterday
in that Newtown Lane newspaper store I don't yet know the name of.
                    Stay with me, A.D. Don't blow. Scout out that bed. Go find

tennis instead of squash mates, surfboarders, volley ball boys
    to play with. I know you will, before long-- maybe among the lifeguards--
big, cool-coned, straight-hipped, stander-on-one-finger, strong.

FIVE HORSES

Midday, midsummer, the field is watercolor green.
  In the center, slats of an open paddock frame.
  A rusty bathtub for water trough in foreground shade.
   Five horses-- two brown, two pinto, one a buckskin-- wade

     the wide green. They are made short by the stature
    of the grass-- hoofs and half their muzzles unseen.
   They keep the composition balanced by their ease
  and placement. On a rectangle of sun, the two brown
 backs, like polished tables, solid, reddish rove.

      The black-on-whites, turned hinders to the wood,
      necks down, feel a slow breeze drag the scarves
       of their manes aslant. One's whole head is a dark hood
        through which the ears, unpainted, point. The other's a mare
         with astonishing blue eyes, and all blond, except for a pale

    tan patch over stifle and loin. The buckskin, youngest,
   crops in shade alone, tail thrown over tawny rump
 in a constant feathery rotar against flies.
They move and munch so gradually, the scene
seems not to change: clean colors outlined on mat-green,

      under a horizontal wash of steady blue
       that ink-sharp, darker swallows, distant, dip into.
       That pasture was the end of one of our walks.
       We brought carrots that we broke and passed
        on the flats of our hands, to the lips of Buck and Blue,

    to Spook, Brown I and Brown II, who nipped and jostled
   each other over the gate to get them.
They'd wait while we stroked their forelocks and smooth jaws.
I could look into the square pupils of the palfrey, Blue,
her underlip and nostrils, like a rabbit's, pink.

      Pied spots, as on a cheetah, showed faint under the hair
       of Buck, your horse: you liked him best.
        Close up, we rubbed the ragged streaks and stars on their
         foreheads and chests, slapped their muscular necks,
          while they nudged us, snuffling our pockets for more.

    Now we've gone past summer and the green field, but I could draw
   their profiles, so distinguished the five faces stay in view,
 leaning over the gate boards toward our coming,
waiting for carrots, staring, yearning in a row.

HOW EVERYTHING HAPPENS (Based on a study of the Wave)


```
                                                           happen.
                                                     to
                                                up
                                        stacking
                                    is
                            something
When nothing is happening


When it happens
                something
                        pulls
                            back
                                not
                                    to
                                        happen.




When                                    has happened.
     pulling back          stacking up
                  happens


          has happened                              stacks up.
When it              something              nothing
                           pulls back while




Then nothing is happening.


                                  happens.
                              and
                        forward
                    pushes
                up
            stacks
        something
Then
```

A PAIR

                              A he
                          and she,
                      prowed upstream,
                    soot-brown
                      necks,
                    bills the green
                 of spring
                 asparagus,

              heads
           proud figure-
        heads for the boat-
        bodies, smooth
     hulls on feathered   the two,
water,   browed with light,
                                          steer ashore,
                                            rise; four
                                                web-
                                         paddles pigeon-
                                                 toe it
                                           to the reeds;

                                                  he
                                           walks first,
                                           proud, prowed
                                           as when light-
                                           browed, swimming,
                                                   he leads

                                                             71

CAMOUFLEUR

Walked in the swamp   His cheek vermilion
A dazzling prince
Neck-band white   Cape he trailed
Metallic mottled
Over rain-rotted leaves   Wet mud reflected
Waded olive water
His opulent gear   Pillars of the reeds
Parted the strawgold
Brilliance   Made him disappear

BEGINNING TO SQUALL

A Buoy like a man in a red sou'wester
is uP to the toP of its Boots in the water
 leaning to warn a Blue Boat

    that, BoBBing and shrugging, is nodding "No,"
        till a strong wave comes and it shivers "Yes."
            The white and the green Boats are quiBBling, too.
                What is it they don't want to do?

The Bay goes on Bouncing anchor floats,
their colors tennis and tangerine.
Two ruffled gulls laughing are laughing gulls,
 a finial Pair on the gray Pilings.

    Now the Boats are Buttoning slickers on
        which resemBle little tents.
            The Buoy is jumPing uP and down
                showing a Black Belt stenciled "1."

A yellow Boat's last to lower sail
to wraP like a Bandage around the Boom.
  Blades are sharPening in the water
            that Brightens while the sky goes duller.

The Boat Stave

Today while a steamshovel rooted in the cove,
leveling a parking lot for the new nightclub,
and a plane drilled between clean clouds

in the October sky, and the flags
on the yachts tied in the basin popped
in a stiff breeze, I watched my footsteps mark

the sand by the tideline. Some hollow horseshoe
    crabshells scuttled there, given motion by the waves.
    I threw a plank back to the waves that they'd

        thrown up, a sun-dried sea-swollen stave
        from a broken dinghy,
        one end square, one pointed, painted green--

        then became so conscious
        of its fate my attention snagged,
        could not get off the hook of its experience,

    for I had launched a subject of the waves
    I could not leave until completed.
    Easily it skipped them, putting out,

prow-end topping every smack and swell,
and kept its surface dry, and looked to float
beyond the jetty head, and so be loose,

    exchange the stasis of the beach for unconceived
    fluidities and agitations. It set sail
    by the luck of its construction:

        Lighter than the forceful waves, it surmounted
        their shove; yet, heavier, steadier than
        the hollows they scooped behind them,

        it used their crested threats for coasting free,
        unsplashed by even a drop of spray,
        was casual master

    of the inconsistent element it rode.
    But there was a bias to the moving sea.
    Though the growth and motion of each wave was arbitrary,

the total spread, of which each crease was part--
the outward hem lying flat by the wall of sky
at the dim blue other end of the bed of the bay--

was being flung, it seemed, by some distant will.
    Though devious and shifty in detail,
    the whole expanse reiterated constancy

and purpose. So, just as the arrowy end of the plank
on a peak of a wave made a confident leap
that would clear the final shoal,

    a little sideways breaker nudged it enough
      to turn it broadside. Then a swifter slap
      from a stronger comber brought it back,

        erasing yards of its piecemeal progress with one push.
          Yet the stave turned point to the tide, and tried again--
            though not as buoyant, for it had got soaked.

          But, arrogance undamaged, it conveyed
            itself again over obstacle waves, a courageous ski--
            not noticing, since turned from shore,

          that the swells it conquered slid in at a slant--
          and that while it met them head on, it was borne
          closer to shore and shunted down the coast.

    Now a bulge-- a series of them, for a pulse
      quickened in the tide-- without resistance lifted
    up the stave, flipped it over twice, and dumped it

rudely in the shallows. It scraped
on sand. And so it was put back--
not at the place of its first effort--

    a greater disgrace than that--
      at before the birth
        of balance, pride, intention, enterprise.

        It changed its hope and goal, and I changed
          my ambition. Not the open sea--
          escape into the rough, the wide unknown, and unpredictability--

        but rescue, return, and rest--
          station, release from influence-- became my hope
        for the green painted, broken slat, once part of a boat.

    Its trials to come ashore the cold
      will of the waves thwarted more capriciously
    than its assays into adventure made before,

and each chance it took to dig with its bent spike
a grip in the salvage of pebbles and weed and shell
  was teasingly, tirelessly outwitted

    by dragouts and dousings, slammings and tuggings
      of the punishing sea. Until, of its own impulse, the sea
        decided to let be,

and lifted and laid, lifted and laid
   the plank inert on sand. At tide turn,
 such the unalterable compulsion of the sea,

it had to turn
its back and rumple its bed
toward the other edge, the farther side of the spread.

 I watched my footsteps mark the sand
   by the tide-line. The steamshovel rooting in the cove
   had leveled a parking lot for the new nightclub.

    The launch from the yacht basin whooshed around the end
       of the pier, toward a sailboat with dropped anchor there,
        whose claxon and flipping flag

          signaled for pick-up. The men with mallets had finished.
          sinking posts by the gangplank entrance
          of the abandoned boat, ballasted with cement

         and painted green and black,
          furnished with paneled bar and dining deck.
        I watched them hang a varnished sign between the posts,

  and letter the name: "The Ark." Tomorrow
I must come
out again into the sun,

 and mark the sand, and
   find my plank.
     for its destiny's not done.

The Blue Bottle

"Go
to the other
shore
and return"
I wrote
in a note
to the bottle
and put it in it.
It kept it
dry.
I
could see
through
the blue
bottle blue
note paper
with blue ink
words.
The cork was tight.
It might
make it.
Blue wavelets let
it go
began to
take it.
Oh
it hobbled
beyond the jetty
rocks barnacled
and snailed.
It bobbled
snagged
on a crag
wagged
with its butt
end butted
but sailed
so far that
its glass
had to pass
for glitter
among glitters
on the flat
glass
of the bay
and my
eye-
glass.

Baited
with
words
and weighted
I thought
"It will get away.
Get away
with it" I
thought
watching
the laps
the lapse
listening
to the lisp
the lips
of the bay-
mouth
making shore
making sure
every rock got
rounded
a little more
today
every pebble
pounded
brought
to ground
and rounded
to be gritted
to a grain
someday
some sum-day
to be mounded
into rock again.
Some fishermen
were fishing
with little
fishes hooked
to hook
bigger fish.
And some they caught
and cooked.
And some they
put on bigger
hooks to get
bigger fishes yet.
And all day
the bay

smacked
its lips big
and little
rocking big and
little ships
that smacked
and rocked like
oyster crackers
in a dish.
The tide was either
going out or it
was coming in.
Not for an in-
stant could it stop
since its pulse compells
it and since
the symdrom swells.
Since syn-rhythm
rules all motion
and motion makes
erosion
all that's munched
apart and
swallowed
shifts collects is
heaped and hollowed
heaped and
hollowed heaped
and hollowed.
All
the little
waves I
followed
out to where my
bottle wallowed.
I was sure sure sure
I was shore shore
it would endure endure
would obey obey
internal pulsion pulsion
of the bay
would turn turn
return return
with the turn- turn- turn-
ing glassy floor
that bore
it for
it wore
internal or-
der at its core.
Constantly my
eye

did pass
over blue
looking with blue
for bluer
blue
on the bottle-blue
bay-glass.
When tide re-
turned
when shore re-
stored
my bottle's envelope
of glass
would be re-versed
even though
its core
burst.
First
erosion
then corrosion
then assemblage.
It would be
nursed
again to
vessel-shape
transparent float
hard hollow
bladder
transferred transplant
holder of my note.
In what
language then
the words the words within
its throat?
What answer? What
other-colored
ink?
My
blue eye
thinking thinking
blinked.
My eye my
I
lost link
with the blue chink
with crinkled
wavelets-lets-lets
let it rising
racing wrinkling
falling
be swallowed
in that inkling

let it sink.

The Stick

The stick is subject to the waves. The waves are subject to
the sea. The sea is subject to its frame. And that
is fixed, or seems to be.

What is it that the stick can do? Can tell the sky, "I
dip, I float. When a wave runs under me, I pretend
I am a boat. And the steersman and
the crew, and the cargo, compass, map. With
a notion of the shore.
I carry all within my lap."

And when a wave runs over it, what is it that the
stick decides? "From your bottom,
cruel sea, you have torn me with your
tides. I am a sliver from some boat, once
swallowed to its water-deep. Why
am I shifted, broken, lost? Let me down, my
rest to keep."

The sea is subject to its frame.
The waves are subject to the sea. The
stick is subject to the waves.
Or does it only seem to be?

What if the stick be washed ashore,
and, gnawed by wind, scoured
by sand, be taken up with other
sticks, into a hand? On some
predicated day, here is what
the stick might say:

"Inside my border, a green
sea flows, that while it
flows is still. A white
wall is around me,
where I am fixed by
someone's will,
who made my shape
into a frame,
and in
this corner
drew
his
name."

```
                          F
                          I
                          R
                          E
                    I S L A N D

                    The Milky Way
                  above, the milky
                  waves beside,
                when the sand is night
                the sea is galaxy.
                The unseparate stars
              mark a twining coast
            with phosphorescent
        surf
      in the black sky's trough.
    Perhaps we walk on black
  star ash, and watch
the milks of light foam forward, swish and spill
      while other watchers, out
        walking in their white
        great
            swerve,
              gather
                  our
                    low
                      spark,
                      our little Way
                        the dark
                        glitter
                        in
                          their
                          s
                            i
                              g
                                h
                                  t
                                  .
```

STONE GULLETS

```
Stone gullets among    Inrush   Feed   Backsuck and

The boulders swallow  Outburst   Hugh engorgements   Swallow

In gulps the sea   Tide crams jagged   Smacks snorts chuckups   Follow

   In urgent thirst   Jaws the hollow   Insurge   Hollow

Gushing evacuations follow   Jetty it must   Outpush   Greed
```

SEEING JUPITER

A chair was placed
upon the lawn
In cloak of wind

          and shadow I
          sat and bent
   my eye upon a rim

of dark that glittered
up to open heaven
In the cup

               a worn dime
          size of an iris
          of anyone's eye

Flat cold lost found
coin of enormous time
Some small change

          around it three
little bits swirled or
     else my ragged eye

with wind swung
In the black pocket
behind that blank

   hung hidden a fourth
          moon dot smarting
as if beneath my tongue

A dreg of ancient mint
My retina tasted
light how long dead?

          My hair thrashed
Enlarged upon the lawn
     my chair I sat in

that wind and shadow
bent had slid
an inch toward dawn

                    ZERO
                IN THE COVE

            The waves have frozen
              in their tracks and turned
          to snow, and into ice

                    the snow has turned, become
          the shore. Where in soft
                            summer sand burned by

        water flat, paralytic
                            breakers stand hurled
          into a ridge of ice. Ice

                        fattens about the poles
          that told the tide.
                        Their two shadows point

        out stiff behind them on a dead
                    floor, thickened and too rough
          for light to glass,

                    as if the moon were drained
            of power, and water
                    were unknown. The cove

            is locked, a still
                chest. Depth itself has
                        died with its
                    reflection
                            lost.

THE
SUNBIRD
SETTLES
TO ITS
NEST

Boys are swimming
through the sun's tail
which is switched
by abrasive waves dyed
flamingo. The head

of the sun is cardinal
from the ears down.
Its pate is pink.
Oh, as I wrote
that, a flush spread

to the hairline.
the chin's no longer
there. The tail
on the waves is sliced
with purple. Oiled ibis-

feathered swells
make it fan
out like a peacock's
But slowly drooped
and narrowed, it drags

west. The boys'
heads are hubs
for scintillating
circles. Their arms plough
a waterfield of eyes.

The peckered scalp
is melting, there goes
the last capfeather
of faint red down down.
Down. The boys come up

almost black.
They flip wet off
by the green-haired rocks,
behind them embered
a phoenix crown.

ROCKY POINT

                    The mainland
looks much smaller than the island,
                    and faint,

        implying thinner paint
            brushed in last
            as background,

            so not as real.
        Here is the present,
        over there, the past.

                Hard to feel
        how it's the larger body.
            That dream-haze

                blue and green,
                    a low wave
                    of land,

                is not clear,
        or as solid as the water
                    in between

                it and the rocky
                    point I stand
        on. That's lifesized,

well-detailed with sunlit trees.
                    The island
is much bigger than the mainland.

                    This shore
            is foreground. Why
        have a figure with its back

                turned, focused
                    on a streak
        in the distance, a coast

                it can't make out?
        (Even the sun forgets
                on foggy days.)

        But that's the larger body,
            that's a fact--
            and would be again if I

        were over there. Packed
            with central life, it's the torso
            this, at best, a leg.

        No. A toe.
            Well, even that is inexact.
            If I think of the whole

        body: what was vast
            in retrospect, small
            now, and thin in

        the blue of forget,
            it was, is, but a hand's
            breadth.   And

        an island. All
            that's earth is,
            on the world's whirled

        wavedrop.
            And this now present outcrop
            (that a magnified

        wave grapples,
            every fingernail
            of foam real

        to my thirsty eye--
            I on a cliff before
            the foreground--

        the brush can't paint itself--)
            is but a hair.
            But oh it's mainland,

        it's the moment's
            ground I stand
            on. It is fair.

85

A NOTE ABOUT ICONOGRAPHS

To have material and mold evolve together and become a symbiotic whole. To cause an instant object-to-eye encounter with each poem even before it is read word-after-word. To have simultaneity as well as sequence. To make an existence in space, as well as in time, for the poem. These have been, I suppose, the impulses behind the typed shapes and frames invented for this collection.

I call the poems Iconographs with such dictionary derivations in mind as these:

icon   "a symbol hardly distinguished from the object symbolized"

icono- from the Greek eikonos meaning "image" or "likeness"

graph   "diagram" or "system of connections or interrelations"

-graph from the Greek graphé meaning "carve"..."indicating the instrument as well as the written product of the instrument"

Also, this comment on "The Art of the Middle Ages" (Columbia Encyclopedia, 3rd Edition) helped me choose the title:

"...(It) was governed by a kind of sacred mathematics, in which position, grouping, symmetry, and number were of extraordinary importance and were themselves an integral part of the iconography. From earliest times it has likewise been a symbolic code, showing men one thing and inviting them to see in it the figure of another..."

I suppose that these were my aims. But I come to definition and direction only afterwards. It has always been my tendency to let each poem "make itself"--to develop, in process of becoming, its own individual physique. Maybe this is why, once the texts were fixed, I have wanted to give for each an individual arrangement in the space of the page.

I have not meant the poems to depend upon, or depend from, their shapes or their frames; these were thought of only after the whole language structure and behavior was complete in each instance. What the poems say or show, their way of doing it with language, is the main thing.

Poetry is made with words of a language. And we say, "But, of course." It is just this "matter of course" that poetry holds to the nostrils, sticks into the ears, puts on the tongue, flashes into the eyes of anyone who comes to meet it. It is done with words; with their combination--sometimes with their unstringing. If so, it is in order to make the mind re-member (by dismemberment) the elements, the smallest particles, ventricles, radicals, down to, or into, the Grain--the buried grain of language on which depends the transfer and expansion of consciousness-- of Sense. And no grain, of sense, without sensation. To sense then becomes to make sense.

With the physical senses we meet the world and each other --a world of objects, human and otherwise, where words on a page are objects, too. The first instrument to make contact, it seems to me, and the quickest to report it, is the eye. The poems in Iconographs, with their profiles, or space patterns, or other graphic emphases, signal that they are to be seen, as well as read and heard, I suppose.

May Swenson

ABOUT THE AUTHOR

ICONOGRAPHS is May Swenson's sixth published book of poems. She is Utah-born, but her main scene has been New York City until recently; she now lives in an "Adirondack shack" overlooking Long Island Sound at Sea Cliff, N.Y. After the printing of HALF SUN HALF SLEEP (1967) some fellow poets and the press had the following to say about her work:

"...(It) often appears to be proceeding calmly, just descriptive and accurate, but then suddenly it opens into something that looms beyond the material, something that impends and implies... her way is to define things, but the definitions have a stealthy trend..." WILLIAM STAFFORD in Poetry.

"...has a wholesome, earthy eroticism, wit and a love for experiment with forms, including typographical games that she manages to justify..." EDMUND FULLER in The Wall Street Journal.

"May Swenson leaps to the love of language and has a ball... is very much in the high baroque fashion of our time, and so much at home in it as to be one of its masters." KARL SHAPIRO in The New York Times Book Review.

"The publication of a volume of new poems by May Swenson is a happy and important event... Her remarkable capacity for the exact impression, her almost Oriental style with its precise, though often bizarre, imagery, and her enormous skill in many shapes and forms has produced an exquisite craftsman..." HOLGAR LUNDBERGH in The American Swedish Monthly.

"Through her language she probes existence, takes what is apart (and not in a surrealistic, but in a scientific way that becomes through accuracy seemingly metaphysical) puts it together again... it then exists." HARRIET ZINNES in Prairie Schooner.

"...the visual physical arrangement is not related to form alone. It reflects the careful observation, the respect for the whole range of the senses... Her poems are not limited to linear time; they are patterns in space as well. The shaped poem represents... the aesthetic need for structure, a need met in other poets by the formal stanza or the syllabic or metric line. The enclosing of the poem within spacial boundaries... is especially appropriate... The territory May Swenson has invaded and penetrated more deeply than other moderns is that of the perceptible." ANN STANFORD in Southern Review.

"(She is) so possessed, now, of the means of her identity that the ritual, spellbinding, litaneutical elements of her art have grown consistent, even coincident, with her temporal, conditioned, suffering experience, and seem... no more than natural." RICHARD HOWARD in Alone With America, Essays on the Art of Poetry in the United States since 1950.

Honors to the poet include a Brandeis University Creative Arts Award & Citation, the Distinguished Service Gold Medal from Utah State University, the PSA Shelley Memorial Award and the Bryn Mawr College Donnelly Fellowship. She was elected to membership in the National Institute of Arts and Letters 1970.